Common Ancestry

For My kindred Roberta
I reach inside myself
for words to express what
has been and still seems
unsayable. This inscription
is an overdue attempt at
telling you how much
I admire and appreciate
you. Thank you
Sojourner
~ Today ~

MILLE GRAZIE PRESS CHAPBOOK SERIES • 8

ALSO BY SOJOURNER KINCAID ROLLE

MURMURINGS OF AN OPEN HEART
OUR STRENGTH WILL GROW
THE MELLOW YELLOW GLOBAL UMBRELLA
A HAND REACHED OUT
BETWEEN US

Common Ancestry

Sojourner Kincaid Rolle

MILLE GRAZIE PRESS
Santa Barbara

Published by Mille Grazie Press
PO Box 92023, Santa Barbara, California 93190

Grateful acknowledgment is made to the editors of
the following publications and on-line magazines in
which some of these poems first appeared:

*Afrigeneas, ArtDirect, California Quarterly, CMP
Newsletter, California State Poetry Society Poetry Letter,
Earthwords, The Santa Barbara Independent,* and *The
Geography of Home* (Heyday Books)

Cover photo: Carruth D. Kincaid, ca. 1915

Cover Design by Laura Davison

ISBN 1-890887-06-4

First Edition

Remembering my grandmother and mother,
Mrs. Carruth D. Kincaid,
a matriarch whose life inspires mine
1900 - 1997

CONTENTS

BLOSSOMING

We speak our names
in no particular order
beginning slow up front

perhaps where the planting began
proceeding in order of rows
then popping up spontaneously

Reaching into ourselves
propelling the thrust of sound
We splay the syllables like petals

Each speaking a solo blossoming

TUBEROSE

The taupe tuberose
mauve-tinged, tall
plump with fragrant pistils
sweet like its sisters
Honeysuckle Jasmine Plumeria
rich aromatic memory
permeates the distal air
carries me back
to my southern comfort
takes me dancing
on Hawaii's fragrant reef
sends me swimming
in Oaxaca's moonlit waters
keeps me running
'long Oregon's sea-swept shores
leaves me basking
in Calafia's Morning Glory

ZACA

*...Therefore the way of the soul in search
of its lost father...leads to the water,
to the dark mirror that lies at the bottom.*

Carl Jung

The mountain   obsidian   shale
cups this green water
in the palm of its oddly shaped hand

Mountain   immovable   ageless
harboring sage and chaparral trails
where Chumash elders roam

Mountain   with sphinx gaze
watching a million tides recede
watching the endless trek and settle

The Seraphim whisper
Echoes dance among the willows
looping the angelic harmony

The lake   ancient as the runted hills
gathers the oldest secrets of the valley
close to its cleavage

Open to any soul questing
touching bottom   a costly discovery
deep in the quiet place

THE BLUE ROCK

This blue stone
once lay like any other pebble
on a rock-infested beach.
Now it warms my palm.
A tiny remembrance
of a day by the sea
and my small vow.

This rock
once lay in the shadow of Diablo
near groves
where sojourning monarchs suckle;
near roads
where guardians of the earth stood
and were arrested.

I lie in the same loam
wallowing among the blue rocks
awaiting the gritty water
the sacred cleansing
sanding my body
smoothing my spirit
preparing for my watch.

THE BIRDS' REFUGE

It was solitary and serene
Wild and unordered
Somebody else's domain

The Canada geese were always friendly
approaching cars in large gaggles
accepting from human hands

Sparrows dotted the wet earth
Pigeons strolled freely
Killdeer hopped beneath the tangled brush

Eggs were laid and hatched in the tall wheat grass
California scrub oaks sprawled full with acorn
calling blue jay and red-headed woodpeckers

One could kneel at water's edge
and commune with the cormorant

It was once that way

ONE

On the promontory
one's own vista
the world before and behind
one questions not
the ebb and flow of tides
nor the heave and hammer of waves
rather the gnashing and gnarling about

the battering
why the loosed whip
when the belly flesh or naked back
lies exposed to the warming sun

what urges inspire a massacre
and why do we sun ourselves
at the juncture of pain

In mating we scream
in childbirth we scream

but when the peace of age descends
we seek safe havens
where sharp jagged edges cannot reach
We place our hearts in velvet cages
where pointed shards cannot touch
we live in visible safety
where only soft love can approach
then we understand

the dawn
the heat of the midday sun
the afternoon
clouds and sunset
and in evening
peace
flows gently
from bay to bay

BUTTERFLY BEACH

On Butterfly Beach
Columns gently styled
Like grecian urns
grace the stretchway

Hold subtle
sway for ocean swells
Sea gulls glide
along the boulevard

Blue dockers stroll
in tennis whites
golfing greens
yachting yellow

Taupe shore
stretches under the foam
Tiny white shells
litter the smoothed wet sand

Walking dogs
chase frisbies
thrown along
the littoral

The lonely
observing the tides
wait for dinner

AN OLD SONG

I have no new voice
it is the same old voice
the voice of my mother
calling
for her daughter
captive of kaleidoscopic mirrors
the voice of her mother crying
for her daughters
lost
in the mill village
singing for the hill people
dancing for nickels

Old as the voice of her
mother screaming for
daughters taller than
herself   tall as the
Carolina pines   taller
than her predators
tall enough to speak
above heads of
inferiors   old as
the voice of her mother
singing from the deep
recesses of her humming
heart   deep where
the memory began
to be played over
for the forgetting

IN THIS TIME

Remembering the Amistad & David Walker's Appeal, 1839

In every reckoning hour
We plea to the God of our fathers, the Jesus of our mothers
Beckoning the angels

In same old voice
We call down our ancestors from the beginning of time
Counting ourselves in their number

In the moments before dawn
We mimic the soft sigh of our mothers
crying out for daughters lost in the great wood

In the twilight
We echo the bold tones of our fathers
bellowing to sons of sons floundering in the crosscurrents

Rise up with unflinching determination
Emerge from the darkened wood
Free yourself from the sucking flood

In the dark of ages night
Expose the hell of bondage to the gazing world
Strike a blow for freedom

Speak with an old voice
Light a new light
Rise Up!

COMMON ANCESTRY

He could remember the whip marks
on his grandmother's beautiful back

Furrows burned in by leather straps
Edges serrated like brutal knives

Thick shiny keloids shaped
like the grooved leaves of the kentia palm

She could remember the wrinkles
on her grandmother's beautiful face

Creases across her forehead
Crinkled hair, wet with menopause sweat

Whimpers of anguish escaping her tight lips

Her eyes stained red with deep memory

EVERGLADE HALLELUJAH

Hosannas for the stalwart Seminole
Hiding slaves in tall marsh grasses
Leading battered bodies bloodied
Into an intricate maze of streams

Can you hear a mother's mantra
Soothing swaddled bone near breast
Guide me o' my unseen Jesus
Lead me on to heaven's rest

Silent waters steady rushing
Niger's issue steady treading
Crossing Jordan's dangerous eddy
Risking death at freedom's shore

Listen for the savior's signal
Warrior's whistling 'call of loon'
Tall marsh grasses waving gently
Sweet bye morning everglade

THE MATRIARCH

Like finely chiseled leather
forming symmetrical patterns,
soft furls drape her muscle
gristle and marrow-rich slender bones.
Still supple like soft ground,
gentle crevices hold ageless secrets.

Like tributaries of the Euphrates,
vibrant blood-pulsing veins
throb beneath their weathered binding
wending their course
throughout the universal network,
turning the old to the new.

Like the planetary clock,
her heart mirrors strong with conviction
sending code words for a dynasty.
Seed-cells double quadruple infinity
offspring branch uncountable tendrils
reared and set free.

Manifesting the vision of the Matriarch.

THE PENDULUM

I listen to the souls of my brothers
and hear the deep beat of tension.

The world churning the head turning
the slow tennis dance of their eyes
back to Eden back to forever
in context no note forgotten
rhythm accentuated in their cry.
How in the holy ghost can heaven
stand the gruesomeness?

Vision within without
raw flesh revealed reveled
pummeled puffy pink
red needing assuage
absorbing absolving ablution
What of earth can giant hills of
time contain? Hard rock fused of
paused clay? Sacred space sentient
sonorous sensuous?

I look into the souls of my brothers
and see the deep set of their hearts.

CHIAROSCURO
on cleaning the Sistine Chapel frescoes

Ironic that the truth
should be sought
on the shoulder of Eve

The human form
melancholy draped
like second skin

Articulated contours
confluent dimensions
the lavish look

More shadow
less brightness
an uneasy light

As the workers cleaned
color no one had seen
emerged alert

Glue glazed layers
once transparent
fell away revealing

Golden violet
grazed with white
luminescence shimmering

AT FIFTY

I have learned to make good lemonade
as well as to savor the moments of co-habitation
when being there is a welcome respite from the churning
world.

I have seen the morning sun rise triumphantly
over a meadow above a stand of vibrant trees
reaching a victorious ascension...and infinite.

I have foraged into fields of blackberries
risking snakebites and enduring thorn pricks
purple-black juice stained my fingers and my tongue
and my bucket was filled to brimming,

And in the heat of day, I have wiped sweat from my
forehead.

I have waded through breast-deep pools on
cool-sided mountains nearly touching dream vistas in the
nearby sky.

I have walked the wilderness path at twilight as ground
creatures scurry to their evening roosts and the red sun
singes the world.

I have leaned forward atop the peak
viewing the showering dance of meteors floating through
time bound space burning their last embers and in their
moment of extinction flashing their brilliance in the
universe.

I have walked across the dampened stand at midnight while foaming white waves clashed against the littoral then sliding gently back into the sea leaving silver speckles in their wake.

I have seen this day rise and recede blending steplessly into tomorrow.

IN THE PASEO

The poet sits
her back to a perfectly fitting corner
looking out on the paseo world.
tourist families posing for snapshots
lovers languishing in oblivion beneath the jacarandas
vendors kitsch from pushcarts tucked among the palms
certainly a time for writing
from the purple.

Shoppers scurry past.
The poet contemplates the seeming absence of waifs;
looking upward, spies their dusty cherubic faces
craftily carved beneath the red tile roofs.
Real beggars are not allowed here.
Invisible barriers maintain the strict monotony.
Wistful dreamers stalk the yellow hibiscus
while big broad women lick their sugar cones.

Across the street, a cluster of vagabonds
Street people, nature lovers, runaways and other
nonconforming linger in the permanence of transience
Frisbee hacky-sack a few guitars
poets searching for their voice among the discarded
The banished King Carlos floats in ethereality
holding court despite impertinent usurpations,
bowling balls and urinals.

She senses some smattering of community
in this walk-through world.

She contemplates contemporary art
peruses the bill of players
ponders the tabloid marquee.
She remembers it as before — a dead-end street.
She knew of other dead-ends, alleys, and outlets;
now each way was strewn with bougainvillea.

THE MEDIATOR

for William Stafford

dwells in the light where no trees
hide the heart and hoists high
the banner of honorable intention
and conscientious objection.

claims the central path
peacemaker
a narrow corridor between opposites

makes pilgrimage into dark and difficult woods
wearing accouterments of courage:
soft-soled shoes, velvet gloves,
a vest of iron will;

navigates jagged parallel terrain
carrying shock absorbing paraphernalia
picking open curious fissures
risking the explosion of live warheads;

understands the many tones of other
and speaks in a universal tongue;

carries short-term palliatives
and lasting conciliation;

dances with a saint's vigor;

flames eternal on the narrow path.

HYPOCRISY

Morning of day so filled with light
Scarlet sunset portends the night
Darkness falls as if by right

Forgiveness and vengeance dwell as one

What love the hand drawn back

What faith the snarled mouth

Sword sheltered in Peace

Is day the only time for sight

Night comes again and again

Moonlight brushes away the dark

SINS OF TIME AT MILLENNIUM'S MARK

Confronting the undead at dawn
Reveille's trumpet echoing
Mnemosyne's daughters stand mute
My task is to read from the scroll

    Osiris's dismemberment
    Ishmael's abandonment
    John's beheading
    Joan's burning

    Ethiopia's enslavement
    India's colonization
    Armenia's slaughter
    Hiroshima's immolation

    The Inquisition
    The Trail of Tears
    The Holocaust
    The Disappeared

    Tibet's displacement
    Cambodia's killing
    Rwanda's destruction
    Bosnia's genocide

The poised pen at heaven's gate
Collective guilt is written here
Six billion souls in the balance
Remorse the only redemption?

THE RISING

Second wind is a mysterious force
—like second light

Galway Kinnell

At the rounding of each plateau
insinuations of greatness
ennoble the bounding ascent.
Volumes of gentle air

without imposition, ripple the ambiance.
Legions of lodge-pole pines,
evergreen, ever faithful,
lift their arms in perennial salute.

Rimming the majestic plane,
a coronet of mountains.
Above the high sierras,
the silence of light reigns.

LITANY FOR A LOST SOUL

There must be some reason
these things thought, written,
spoken compel themselves to
production for the world to know, see, hear,
Affairs of the spirit no more shielded
from the heel of scorn than flagrant crimes
against the body politic

Is there no sanctity of the private dome
are there no more secrets of the personal realm
will the sacred matter of the mind
go the way of the secret vote, the true
confession, the privileged confidence,
into the public domain

Why search for the sacred
when all life is polluted by the profane
politics of megalomaniacal millionaires
trying to balance their pleasure
with the interest from a billion
bounced checks

Vainless iconoclasts
posturing for a pinned-up portrait
devoid of the succulent essence of
reality long since roasted
on pyres in the round
flames reflected in red eye
flights across a blood-stained sky

Satellites sending
fresh evidence of new frontiers
States altered, conquered, neutered
Age old signals of a new order
Notwithstanding prior claims
disregarded as nostalgia
mere twitchings of the soon to be dead

Soul

THE PALLBEARERS

on viewing Van Gogh's "Wheatfield of Crows"

Morning mists move across the vale.
A phalanx of birds rises from the golden savannah
Keepers of the road from here to there.

It is an ominous thing —

Crows, black, shiny, eyes keen
Hovering above the fields of grain
Cawing at the unseen

The fearful fall sprawling at the gate;
The soul, ready, steps forward
Unto the path.

In blinding wisdom
Spirits of the ascended
Bathe the way.

HANDS IN THE MOTION OF PRAYER

Mottled hands cupped deep
like the pouch of a brown pelican
reach for the bounty of the sea
while crows claw crabs
from web-footed gulls and
soar to perches once claimed
by cooing birds

Hands softened by surf and sand shimmer
like suave salmon flashing a satin coat
stroke the battering waves
cradle the hammered ears of passing argonauts
consort with dolphin and otter
in full view of predators
inviting their touch

Gnarled and pebbled hands
like the barnacled backs of fabled turtles
groveling among the agate and cobalt
Finger-thin pincers mince lifeless
shells and held fast debris
curling into the sworled chambers
teasing out the left behind

Hilled stands of western hemlock
high above the rugged coast
Blunt fingered limbs forming stately portals
house the gentle prayers of crust creatures
soft winds swaying
slowly swirling ribbons twirling
blowing murmured aspirations

Toward the sky

I'M GONNA WRITE

I wish I had more time to be a poet
instead I have poetry endeavors and
peacemaking efforts and service to
the community and love for my family
and a desire to be with my friends,
not to mention shopping to dress and
collect things of my fancy and
synthesizing experiences and seeking
the new. I wish that I had time to
write.

I wish I could recall all that I have lived
instead I work from flashbacks
which float up from fields of nostalgia
reconstructing anecdotal slivers of the past
such as the day JFK was killed
and the murder of Martin Luther King
and the message of the muslims
the ministry of malcolm
and the time I went to Washington
and working in Harlem
and the night the lights went out at the library
I wish I could recall everything
in perfect detail. I must take
more time to write.

I wish you could respect me
for the life I have to give rather
than the life of your expectations

My heart open pours forth the salt
essential to the savory of the soul
my fingers conduct synaptic images
striven for the synchronicity of a
commonly held seance. My being
carries a dynamic created of known
and intuited past and future
I must speak these things together
I must have more time to write.

SPEAKING OF NAMES

We say the names we have been given to carry —
Names of ancestors; our grands and great-grands
Family icons; Dad's favorite sister, Mom's matronly aunt.
We are anointed with the names of the famous
Movie stars, Presidents, the fictional, the sainted.
We are drenched in the perfume of fine names;
Names of biblical intention and historical significance.
We bask in the aura of our name's countenance —
Spend our lives being worthy of its provenance.

And so we have the speaking of names.
Our names mean something to us
Eschewing anonymity and against obscurity,
We send up our mantles, our monikers, our noms de plume —
festooning the universe with a plethora of hand-me-up hopes.
Projecting our aspirations onto stars and comets,
we claim places in the heavens for our namesakes.

PRAISE POEM TO LUCILLE

for Lucille Clifton, on her birthday 1996

We have come to this
you, white-haired, golden-toned
daughter-rich, son-blessed
you, great part our mother,
several parts out sister,
some parts southern,
many parts northern,
your feet planted where your people stood
A glint of Africa abides in your gleaming teeth
a hint of India in your smiling eyes
California riding the shadow
of your lifted brow
We praise the light that shines from you
We celebrate your joy

CATCH LIGHT

The porcelain moon, crested and full,
like a flashlight
gazing into a wooden bowl,

Peers into the valley
giving form to the dark inhabitants
tree, boulder, insect, flora, you — me.

We near, become still, soundlessly respire
peer into the blackness of other
savoring our own ambiguity.

Your face, round like the moon,
belies its twin in contorted shadows
crevices like canyons bend against the night.

What is between us refuses quiet —
laughs at shadows —
jumps, white and uncontained.

I discern the red fire, dancing.
I lean closer, into your mystery —
fearful and magnetized.

Our shadows meld.
Our cloistered souls
embrace.

PEACE GARDEN POEM

my hands stalwart like giant parapets
my fingers
a swallow flock
tethered to Kilamanjaro
a mountain of hope
my swallows race
like spiders spinning silk
a span
the bridge from Hiroshima
the swallows
a graceful choir gliding
sing of sadness
sing of peace
joy is in the illumined village
in every harmonious
melodious beat of wing

I wave my hand
sound sweeps
the vista of time

HEAL

There is that time
when the pronouncements of surgeons
count not nearly as much as a whispered hope
when the fingers wielding scapel
can neither put back nor rejoin.
Herein is the real domain of the creator;
the building of sinew,
the melding of synapse.

We grasp for life.
It is a involuntariness of human
outstretched fingers
reaching into the abyss — risking failure
knowing it is the welding power of love that must
reach into the sinew, across the synapse;
burning white hot,
warming the cooling bed.

A PALL ON THE DAY

These days of elegy
These days heavy and nagged by resignation
These days of counting dead

These days of disclarity
That retching racing of the senses
Ascertaining threat

These days of tragedy
Psyches battered beyond the truth of things
Terror shadowing our spirits

For what good is it
This hell driven horror
This unspeakable sorrow

These days of mass grief
Tearless mourners bite back the awkward flood
Sucking up the pride

These days when love is sad
Lying open like a beached orca
Needing life's great affirming

These days when anger biles up
Like bad food seeking the closest egress
Bitter remains on its path

These days burdened with pall
Blue notes somewhere in the distance
Fog thick air holding our breath

NOTES

page 4:   "The Blue Rock"
Diablo Canyon is near Morro Bay,
California where demonstrators protested
the building of a nuclear power plant.

page 20:   "The Mediator"
Written in memory of poet William
Stafford, 1914 - 1993, a conscientious
objector during World War II, and a
longtime member of the Fellowship of
Reconciliation.

page 22:   "Sins of Time at Millennium's Mark"
Mnemosyne is the goddess of memory,
consort of Zeus, Mother of the Nine Muses
whose task was to tell the legends of the
Greek gods through the arts of poetry,
music, theater and dance.

Photo by Rod Rolle

Sojourner Kincaid Rolle has published five previous chapbooks of poetry. Her poems have appeared in many print journals, including: *California Quarterly, Coffee Press, Squaw Review* and *Café Solo*; as well as the on-line magazines: *ArtDirect, Afrigeneas,* and *Caspita for Kids.* Her work has also been anthologized in *Earthwords* (White Crow Press) and *The Geography of Home: California and the Poetry of Place* (Heyday Books).

Rolle is a founding member of the Santa Barbara Poetry Festival. Since 1991, she has hosted a monthly reading series, "Poets' Night." She has written two dramatic works: "Sweet Home Hallelujah;" and "Jazz at Big John's," which she directed and in which she also performed. For six years, she produced and hosted a popular local cable television show, "Outrageous Women."

Rolle has led creative writing workshops and classes throughout the western United States, including the Yachats Literary Festival in Oregon. She recently edited a collection of writings, *Inner Space*, by participants in her California Arts-In-Corrections classes. She is affiliated with California Poets In The Schools. She also works as a mediator.

MILLE GRAZIE PRESS CHAPBOOK SERIES

1. **Joyce La Mers**, *Grandma Rationalizes an Enthusiasm for Skydiving*

2. **Valentina Gnup-Kruip**, *A Certain Piece of Sky*

3. **Benjamin Borteck**, *Having Accomplished So Little*

4. **Phil Taggart**, *Opium Wars*

5. **Robert Wynne**, *Patterns of Breathing*

6. **Wilma Elizabeth McDaniel**, *Sleeping in a Truck*

7. **Ned Schill**, *Tendrils and Trumpets*

8. **Sojourner Kincaid Rolle**, *Common Ancestry*

9. **Robert Arroyo, Jr.**, *Truant Light*

10. **Paul Willis**, *Poison Oak*

11. **Will Inman**, *you whose eyes open naked into me*

12. **Bettina T. Barrett**, *Heartscape*

Price: $6.00 each

California residents only: add 47¢ sales tax per book

Shipping: $1.00 for the 1st book,
add 50¢ for each additional book

ORDER FROM: Mille Grazie Press
PO Box 92023
Santa Barbara, CA 93190

Make checks payable to **Mille Grazie Press**